GHOST IN
THE CLUB

Published by Metatron
www.onmetatron.com
305-5555 Ave. de Gaspé, Montreal QC H2T 2A3

Copyright © Greg Zorko, 2016
All rights reserved.
ISBN 978-0-9939464-8-6

Editing | Jay Ritchie
Layout and book design | Ashley Opheim
Cover art | Teo Zamudio

First edition
Second printing

We acknowledge the support of the Canada Council for the Arts, which last year invested $153 million to bring the arts to Canadians throughout the country.

Canada Council   Conseil des arts
for the Arts   du Canada

GHOST IN THE CLUB

GREG ZORKO

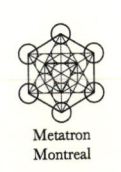

Metatron
Montreal

CONTENTS

Small and Manageable Feelings

gee 9
make sure you stay hydrated 10
brown rice 11
take-out box 12
flower print 14
Cheburashka 16
soapsuds 17
high waisted jeans 19
vision 21
gray pigeon 22
hard-boiled egg 24
Chia Pet 26
toddler 27
information 29
kale 30
fern 31
butterfly hair tie 33
energy efficient light bulb 35
reusable cloth shopping bag 36
smoke cloud emoji 37
drool 38
Pop-Tart 39
raspberry muffins 40
watching cartoons in a blanket fort 41
burrito 42
winter hat 44
weird spirit 45
state park 46
if a baby sees you leave the room it will think you have left the universe 47

Ghost in the Club

Xbox 360　53
DIY haircut　55
bug spray　56
loyalty card　57
Cutthroat Kitchen　58
recycling bin　60
the floor is lava　62
Nerf basketball　63
Ghost in the Club　64
Bananarama　65
Abraham Lincoln　66
glucosamine　67
water vapor　68
blooming onion　69
Robert De Niro　70
evil　72
club sandwich　73
tongue scraper　75
postcard　77
ceramic statue　78
LMFAO　79
lawn gnome　81
amateur　83

SMALL AND MANAGEABLE FEELINGS

gee

i wonder:

what is happening to me?

i feel like a jellyfish

who texted you twice

to make plans for tomorrow,

then wilted on the floor

like a weirdo flower.

make sure you stay hydrated

after i got back from the zoo

you sent me an email

with a link to your Bandcamp account.

now i am eating grape tomatoes

listening to a song you recorded

called, "make sure you stay hydrated"

which is:

a recording of you

reading the Torah

dubbed over the sound of a cat

scratching a maple tree.

brown rice

we have been eating only

vegetarian flautas

for the last two weeks.

you say it's time to "switch it up"

and you come back from the corner store

with orange tea

gummy bears

and seaweed.

with a look of satisfaction

i can't really describe.

take-out box

you yelled at me,

what is this!?!

what is it!?!

pointing to a bruise

on your upper thigh

the shape of the Catholic cemetery

that we went to a few days ago.

i guess a famous person was buried there.

i remember

it was bright out

i was eating a mango,

feeling like a child celebrity.

it was Tuesday afternoon.

"that looks like a squirrel,

or a mailbox"

i said.

flower print

we are driving to the toy store

in a snowstorm

to buy Play-Doh

because

you feel like making something with your hands.

later

you build a demon

with white claws and yellow eyes.

wait for it to solidify

in the "desert biome"

which is on top of the radiator

between the dying cactus

and the gecko action figure.

now

i look at the demon

sometimes

when we are in bed.

it reminds me of how unlike a demon you are.

Cheburashka

i want to send you a four second Snapchat

so you can know at least

that there is a human

who is happy enough to manipulate an electronic device

to point it at their own face

and emote in some way

and who wants that emotion to exist

for a limited time

in the hands of someone else.

soap suds

before i got out of bed

i searched the internet for things

my phone against my body pillow

almost touching my lips.

- how long until an avocado goes bad?

- fancy fancy cheese

- red wine flu cure

- the dangerous ladder of divine ascent

- Chris Farley place of birth

if you can't already tell,

i am liking the point i am at right now,

i am interested in everything that could interest a person.

i have technology.

i have desire.

i am going to the kitchen

to make a bomb-ass chocolate shake.

high waisted jeans

the point of being two separate people

is to share everything.

so

let's feel our feelings

but keep them small and manageable,

apple- or avocado-sized

so we can toss them

across this room.

coming back from the gyro place

we hold hands for a while then stop.

i feel like running away

beyond the place i was going to,

past the theater

and the frat houses

through a hole in the ice

and

into the water.

i will be the world's first

twenty-something baby fish.

vision

i am small and not lonely

the world is a warm pita for me.

i am the chicken, the lettuce and aeoli.

i feel so happy about this

i post things on the internet about the health benefits of raw coconut milk

like a prophet

in the wilderness.

i want the earth to be aware of raw coconut milk.

gray pigeon

together

early morning

eating cereal mix

in the park by the empty fountain

you pass me a peanut

then a cashew,

then another peanut.

and i realize

that i like the way your voice sounds

through four M&Ms.

you explain the plot of a movie

while i wipe crumbs off my leggings

and watch a bug crawl to the center of your Star of David tattoo.

i don't think anyone released an album this year

that is better than listening to

hungover people

walk home in light rain.

hard-boiled egg

you should

stick a fork in me

like a hard-boiled egg.

or

pull apart my body

like a Christ figurine.

today

i wanna feel

like a cow falling over.

i'm already back among the living

when you call me sounding worried

and i tell you,

don't be.

this week i had a fever

so i wasn't just staying in bed

for no reason.

Chia Pet

i know that you aren't playing guitar

you are just

hitting your knuckles against a guitar

and singing

Bruce Springsteen's

"Dancing in the Dark"

but i appreciate the sentiment.

toddler

we play three-on-three basketball which ends in

you bruising your knees

and me

spilling a blue sports drink on my chin. now we are

walking together,

purple and blue,

to the bus stop

where you scold me for looking at my phone too much.

"i am conducting productive research"

i look for:

- population of Indiana

- amount of pizza places in Wisconsin

and other things, i think.

at night

i go to sleep before you.

again

i dream of ways

to easily steal

from certain chain retail stores.

i want to steal six pairs socks.

i want to steal four tons vape juice

i want to steal breakfast cereal

secretly i want to be caught.

information

if you ever find yourself

on a cloud

being pushed by a wind

ascending to the heavens

send me a text

or an email

or something.

kale

you called your best dance move

"forgiving my enemies"

i don't remember it that well

i think

it involved standing on your head.

i am always losing things in the past

like pieces of cheese

in a garbage disposal.

i want to go back there

i want to just sit and do nothing

and watch.

fern

after you tried to scare me

by turning off all of the lights

and

hiding behind the fake tree

by the door

i listened to you chop onions and garlic.

when we were eating falafel

on the couch

and you were never able to explain

how yellow bruises disappear

or

how a feeling can still be a feeling

even if it's empty.

i don't want to get up right now, OK?

toss me the reason you are sad

hand me your confusion about your place on this earth

pass me that thingy

the one you've got in your hand.

butterfly hair tie

you beat me at video games

until my ears hurt.

it's like heaven

for the two days

right after you quit your job

and you still have enough money

to afford peanut butter cups and orange juice

at the cheaper corner store

past the more expensive one.

when you are in the other room i wonder

are you experiencing "cabin fever"?

are you writing "sad boy" poetry?

are you using a lint roller

on your navy blue leggings?

i am wondering these things

and other things too.

energy efficient light bulb

we are at the beach,

which is not really the beach

during winter

with everything frozen.

taking turns

we use our bodies

to slow the wind.

you are wearing a hat

that you knitted.

it took you six months

to knit a picture of a loaf of bread

with the word

"CARBS"

written on it.

reusable cloth shopping bag

one thing we have in common

is that we both have wishes.

i wish that you could dunk a basketball.

i want you to dunk on me

and have the teens at the playground court take a picture of it.

i want to get the picture blown up

poster size

and pin it on your wall

during the night before your birthday

to make you happy in the morning

but for now

i need to work on

more ambitious goals.

smoke cloud emoji

one of my favorite T-shirts got ripped

at the pop show last night.

the band with two singers

wearing ugly Christmas sweaters

with wistful lyrics

about being 19

and doing something on a Wednesday night

like kissing a person

in a snow-covered driveway,

or smoking pot in a jungle gym.

you feel yourself floating towards the moon

or dying

or a combination of both those things,

and all of this makes your stomach

like a kicking baby.

drool

you say to yourself

"today i want a good excuse to feel sad"

at the bus stop with your headphones on

blowing bubbles in gum

to the rhythm of a song.

you feel like using your pinky finger

to draw a picture in the snow.

art for you

was always something you did

instead of changing your life.

on a day when it is foggy as hell

you send me a text

"look out the front window.

how close can i get

until you can see me?"

Pop-Tart

watching pirated films on your computer

i discovered that

i relate to stories

about lonely aliens

being sent to planet earth.

like how yesterday

i felt similar to an alien

when the power went out

and i walked to 7-11

to buy cranberry juice and popcorn.

almost everything was quiet.

i saw the stars and planets

and i thought they looked

totally boring.

raspberry muffins

before going to your best friend's nephew's birthday party

we listen to a lecture

about "the cosmos"

on the internet.

through a chewing gum bubble

you say something

soft and unintelligible

soft like anything that involves feathers.

soft like the part of your ear that is soft.

this is the effect that

no sunlight,

two hours,

and a vague feeling of happiness has on you.

watching cartoons in a blanket fort

when you finish drinking your iced coffee

let's go

listen to your friend's emo band

in a snow bank,

and try not to age

or get closer to dying.

burrito

this morning

i figured out

that you must have thrown up the veggie burrito you had for lunch

and that's why you were talking about chicken wings

when we were walking back

from your cousin's ugly sweater party.

3 a.m.

between the library and the bagel shop

a bird nearly shit on you

you said "wrath of the gods" out loud

and laughed.

too busy

looking for the answers to questions,

staring into the light of your phone

reading about the cause and time of death

of several different famous people

you touch your eyeball and smile.

winter hat

i draw all over myself with crayons,

sharpening them between my teeth.

i think that i am a beautiful

varicolored bird.

when i listen to you in the other room,

your sneakers make a noise.

you light the Justo Juez candle and water the cactus.

i hear your voice get closer to the ceiling.

i'm happy to know you are growing.

the way cornflakes grow in milk.

weird spirit

i am walking into the living room

past the potted fern

when i hear you yell

"prepare for battle!"

you are holding the decorative samurai sword

the one i gave you on New Year's Day

and mounted on the bathroom wall.

you are staring at a cantaloupe

then you break the sword against it.

you look a little disappointed,

you push your nose like a button

and we are let loose from our bodies

like headless fish.

state park

sitting in the tub

hungover vaping

with one of the strawberry bath bombs that you

made the day before.

when i am leaving for work

you close your eyes and say

"don't let me die here,

vaping alone"

but you survived

so that's a good sign.

if a baby sees you leave a room it will think you have left the universe

you sound like a monk

when you say

"tell me your wifi password."

closing your eyes

you think about almost nothing,

and your chest moves

only because it was made to move.

you look a little tired,

either with today

or because of four mimosas.

the password is:

"SORROWIFI"

all caps.

and if you want to know anything else,

if there is a part of me that is far from you

please just ask.

GHOST IN THE CLUB

Xbox 360

the things i would like to do this weekend

include:

having my head karate chopped off,

sticking my tongue out at a flock of geese,

pushing a snowflake off of your nose,

and deciding between a red or black bean burrito.

also,

i want you to grind up my body parts

and process them into vape juice

and then vape the juice while you are walking your dog.

and people will ask you,

"what kind of dog is that?"

and you will say

"it's part beagle part pug"

and different people will ask you

"what kind of juice are you vaping?"

but don't tell them that it is made out of my body

tell them it's Fruit Loops

or waffles

or something else.

DIY hair cut

your new way to cure my hangovers

is to hit me repeatedly on the head

with my grandmother's 1952 edition

of Anna Karenina

while shouting "audiobooks!"

i like spending time together,

i want you to express yourself,

this Saturday

i want everything to turn to dust

and then i want to eat all the dust

and puke it up in my favorite restaurant

so i will have to avoid that place

for like 5 or 6 months

until most of the employees either quit or get fired,

and no one remembers.

bug spray

you talk about your habit

of putting your tongue on cold things

in winter

"it's how i choose to express my love"

when we are coming back from the museum,

breathing in clouds

talking about the circus tent exhibit,

the tiny clown car

and the huge clown cannon.

we hear someone scream

and it is muffled in the snow.

then you punch me on the arm

gently and say

"it's probably just those people

who get drunk at 3:30 p.m."

loyalty card

watched a sped up video

of a sloth eating leaves

with dancehall music playing in the background

and felt

a crippling and physical

sense of jealousy.

Cutthroat Kitchen

we were

drawing on each other

in permanent marker,

triangles and stars,

before the sacred geometry

themed dance party.

we felt holy

and moved like

non-self-conscious people

for like, 2 - 4 hours.

i could hear

vomit hitting ice and pavement

falling in waves

thinking of the beach

and pulling cold air into my lungs.

i wish i had a better memory of this.

recycling bin

good thing

your phone didn't run out of battery

before we finished listening

to Talk Talk's third album

while eating one box of raspberries each.

feeling full now

and seriously ill,

i am looking at the surface of the lake

from your kitchen window

as far as i can see.

i want to go there now.

i'd like to be a lot smaller

so that you will not hear or know me

you will step on me and crush my body

like in *Honey I Shrunk the Kids*.

except nobody was stepped on or died, i think, in *Honey I Shrunk the Kids*.

the floor is lava

let's fill the bathtub

with dirt and potting soil

we can plant

tulips

and maybe sweet potatoes

or

we could make the tub

into a tropical rainforest

with fake plastic

poisonous frogs.

why not?

nobody uses it anyway.

Nerf basketball

u text me

"i am making blueberry pancakes."

and i feel conflicted

because i hate blueberries and love pancakes.

i feel small in my body,

like the last large egg in a carton of twelve.

i would like to leave the door to my apartment open

until moths come in to eat my eyebrows and skin

and bats fly in to eat my bones

and shit all over the place.

i will lose my security deposit.

Ghost in the Club

i go to the club and coat check my entire body.

i record a song with T-Pain

called "Ghost in the Club."

"Ghost in the Club"

becomes the number one song on iTunes

and the most played song on Spotify.

the "Ghost in the Club" dubstep remix

has 500 million views on YouTube.

Justin Bieber asks me to do a collaboration with him for his next album.

i realize,

"fuck,

i am a ghost in the world of spirits,

i can't really even enjoy this."

Bananarama

the moment

when we were at the mall

in a store

and you said

"i don't get it,

it's just a bunch of hats."

Abraham Lincoln

i am sitting against the wall

wiggling my toes

putting on chapstick

and looking at the internet.

you send me a message,

you wrote a haiku.

it goes:

"i am the biggest

fuck up

of all time"

i went into the kitchen,

ate half a carton of strawberries,

i sat down on the floor and wrote

"that is not a haiku."

glucosamine

wearing a summer dress

in bed

when it's 20 degrees outside

and you send me a video

of a raccoon eating cotton candy.

i watch it

in between watching two flowers wilt

in an empty jelly jar

by the window

and listening for something,

idk what.

i spent that entire afternoon

sitting in the light coming through the blinds,

letting it heat up my eyelids

and forehead

trying to become a star.

water vapor

mostly our friendship involved

getting better at ping pong

being hungover in different rooms

and thinking of quick ways to heal our bodies.

we had vague ideas

about resurrection

which we expressed

through playing ten year old video games

and wearing each other's clothes.

when we looked like death,

we did it together.

i bumped my head against a door

that you opened

and you got a black eye

from a baseball we were throwing.

blooming onion

you said,

"hey i heard a pop song last night

and the singer was talking about

'heart strings'

do you have 'heart strings'?"

you poke me in the stomach with your pointer finger twice

you pinch my cheek once

"do you have 'heart strings'?"

Robert De Niro

i found a bunch of

non-expired movie passes

in my sock drawer

so i went to the movies

three times that week.

the first time i cried,

the second time i cried again

the third time i cried.

i was holding a bucket of soda

like a new parent.

feeling vaguely emotional

about sound

and light

in two dimensions.

every time i got back you asked me,

"was it good?"

and i said,

"yeah, it's super good."

i couldn't think of anything more specific.

evil

i don't think

that descending into hell

is anything like

how it is briefly depicted

at the end of *Ghost*

starring Patrick Swayze.

club sandwich

we dress each other.

i put on your blue romper

you put on my Dennis Rodman T-shirt

we do our makeup in the kitchen.

the kitchen still smells

like bagels and curry.

on the way

you spread your arms wide

and send warm air out into the world.

you are involved in every thought of mine.

in the center of my brain there is a path that is peaceful and quiet.

dancing

at the party i heard someone say

that our relationship is like

trying to beat Pokémon Blue Version

with both eyes closed.

tongue scraper

yesterday instead of working

i used Photoshop to put your face over the faces of several pandas.

this is not me wasting time.

this is a scientific method to determine

whether a panda version of you could ever exist.

when we are together

and the only light

is the light that comes

from your phone

and my computer,

we look at old pictures.

me holding a fishing pole.

you next to a Renaissance painting.

i remember that i didn't catch any fish.

"i don't like to kill fish

or even eat them

really."

postcard

do not

yell at me

unless

i am in

serious danger

or

unless you

feel like it.

either way,

it's fine,

whatever.

ceramic statue

i'm sorry.

i never supported your dream

of becoming a famous rapper

i just watched you bob your head

to electronic beats

from a Casio keyboard

in the kitchen

watched you adjust your Chicago Bulls leggings,

stick your tongue out at me

and frown.

i must have been jealous,

well, probably not,

but i feel jealous now.

LMFAO

on Saturday you said

that you didn't want to go ice fishing

because your stomach kind of hurt

and that maybe you got poisoned by that Thai food from three days ago

or from Culver's the day before.

you said "i will see"

and "i just almost choked on a slice of cucumber."

in my room alone

i act superstitious

to feel safe

i take a teddy bear

and balance it on my head.

i think

"this is working,

this is going to work."

lawn gnome

i will only say goodbye

after we have passed the high score in Star Trek pinball

even if it takes

a biblical lifespan,

or a journey from my body

to a spiritual dimension.

i don't care about becoming a ghost,

i think ghosts are cool as hell

like

having no body

being silent

taking energizing naps.

now

in our highly specific dreams

let's remember everything that was good

like when our bodies were caught in doorways,

or on bike racks.

when we were sitting eating fried cheese curds,

the time when it was windy,

and i didn't feel

any stress in my forehead

or kneecaps.

let's send each other the same message at the same time

"i am super hungry wanna go get crepes?"

and if one of us dislikes seeing the other one sad

we're going to have to get over it.

we don't have any choice about that.

amateur

i feel nostalgia now

any time i eat a cheesecake

even though we never ate cheesecake

so maybe this is not "nostalgia"

in a dictionary-definition sense.

i feel that i miss you

slightly less than i should,

and maybe it is snow

melting into a lake

reminding me of that.

Greg Zorko was born in 1990 in upstate New York. He currently lives in Madison, Wisconsin where he writes things and goes to school.

A version of "LMFAO"
appeared in REALITY BEACH.

Versions of "Nerf basketball"
"gray pigeon" and "winter hat"
appeared on ÖMËGÄ.

A version of "DIY hair cut"
appeared in Fog Machine.